YOU CAN DRAW IT!

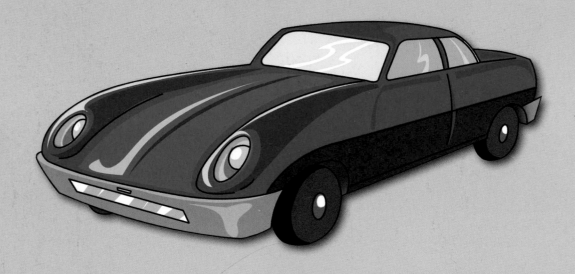

ARCTURUS

This edition published in 2015 by Arcturus Publishing Limited
26/27 Bickels Yard, 151–153 Bermondsey Street,
London SE1 3HA

ISBN: 978-1-78404-511-1
CH004422UK
Supplier 26, Date 0415, Print Run 3816

Artwork: Q2A India
Additional cover artwork: Dynamo Limited
Text: Trevor Cook and Lisa Miles
Editors: Fiona Tulloch and Joe Harris
Cover design: Mike Reynolds and Maki Ryan

Printed in China

Contents

Introduction

This book will show you how to draw lots of different things. In fact, by the time you've learnt all the techniques, you'll be able to draw anything!

You'll see that even the most complicated-looking picture can be recreated by following these simple, step-by-step instructions!

① First choose a photograph of the subject you want to draw.

② Begin by drawing basic outline shapes.

③ Add in a bit more detail. At this stage your subject should start to become recognisable.

④ Add in more details until you've completed your line drawing.

⑤ Colour in your drawing to match the photograph, or pick your own colours.

Materials

Before we start, let's get some materials together.

Gather up your pencils, pens and paintbrushes. Make sure your pencils are sharp!

You can use any smooth, white paper to practise your pencil drawing. Spend some time practising on cheap paper to build up your confidence, saving the nicer paper for your final drawing. If you're going to colour your drawing, start with a strong watercolour paper that will resist wrinkling.

An eraser with a chisel-shaped end is ideal for correcting and removing small bits of your drawing. Use a big, soft eraser after inking to remove all the rough pencil lines.

Compasses draw the best circles.

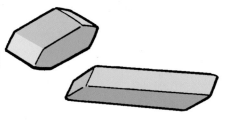

Sometimes we need lines to be very straight and neat. Using a ruler will help with this.

Inking and Colouring

The drawings in this book have been finished with an ink line. You can apply ink with a special felt tip, dipping pen or even a fine brush. The ink must be waterproof if you are going to use water-based paints to colour your picture.

Colour your pictures with felt tips, pencils or paint – it's up to you! If you choose paint, you can use water-based paint like poster paint or gouache.

It is important to pick the right paintbrush for your picture. Use round, pointed ones for fine detail and broad ones for flat areas of colour.

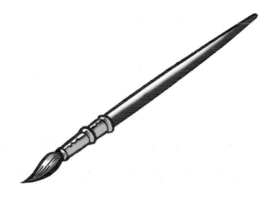

This plump hippo's curves make it quite easy to draw.

Get this rhino's sharp horns just right.

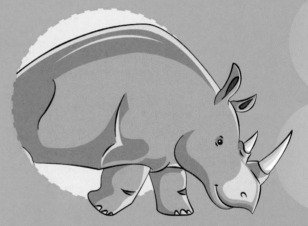

Give this proud gorilla a fierce expression.

This happy penguin is fun to draw.

WILD ANIMALS

These subjects are really wild! Animals are great to draw because they come in all shapes, sizes and colours! This chapter shows you how to draw wild animals that you may not have seen in real life before!

Rhinoceros

Rhinos have excellent hearing. However they cannot see very well.

Some kinds of rhino have one horn. Others have two.

Rhinos have very thick skin.

They can run as fast as a racing bicycle.

FUN FACTS ● FUN FACTS ● FUN FACTS ● FUN FACTS ● FUN FACTS

The rhino is the second largest land animal. Only the elephant is bigger!

1. Draw a body like a big rock.

2. His face is low down.

3. Give him little ears and eyes. Add a strong horn on his nose.

4. Draw his four legs. He's got lumpy knees!

Gorilla

A gorilla is very heavy. He weighs almost as much as three men!

The gorilla is a gentle animal.

His body is covered in lots of black fur.

He can stand on two legs. However he likes to move on all fours.

FUN FACTS ● FUN FACTS ● FUN FACTS ● FUN FACTS ● FUN FACTS

A group of gorillas is called a troop. The leader is a male called a silverback. He has silver hair on his back!

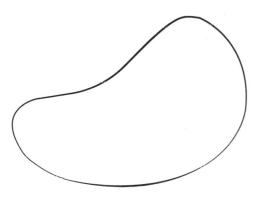

1. Start with the body shape.

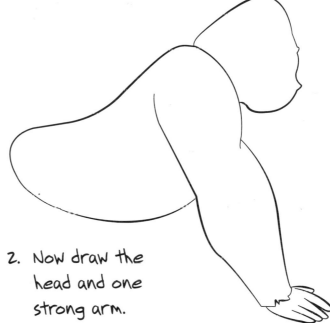

2. Now draw the head and one strong arm.

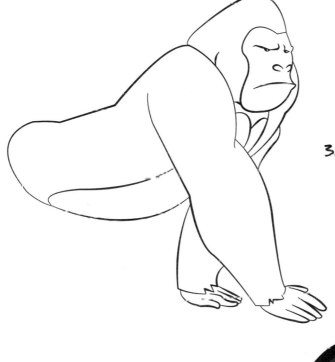

3. Put in the face and the other arm.

4. The back legs are not as big as the arms.

Leopard

The leopard has a spotty coat. She can hide in the trees and grass.

Her long tail helps her to balance.

She has strong legs. She's a fast runner and a good swimmer, too!

She has soft pads on her paws. These help her to walk quietly.

FUN FACTS ● FUN FACTS ● FUN FACTS ● FUN FACTS ● FUN FACTS

A leopard often drags its food up a tree to eat it.
It can pull up to three times its own body weight!

1. Draw this sausage shape.

2. Draw the head with an open mouth.

3. Now add the front legs and tail.

4. Put on her back legs and her special spotty pattern.

Hippopotamus

The hippopotamus spends a lot of time in the river.

His ears, eyes and nose are at the top of his head. The rest of his body can stay underwater.

His skin makes its own special sunscreen!

His mouth opens really wide.

FUN FACTS ● FUN FACTS ● FUN FACTS ● FUN FACTS ● FUN FACTS

The hippopotamus can walk underwater. It can hold its breath for up to five minutes!

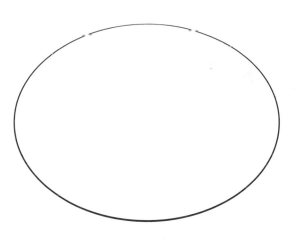

1. First draw this big oval.

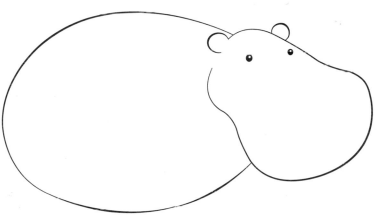

2. Then add his head with little ears and a wide mouth.

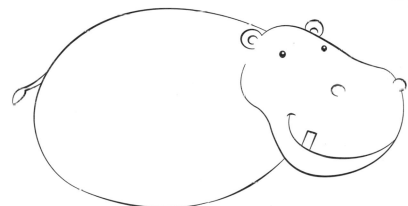

3. He has a little tail.

4. His legs are tiny for such a big body.

Penguin

There are 17 types of penguin. This is a King penguin.

Penguins are birds but they can't fly! They use their wings to swim.

King penguins live in the far south. It's very cold there.

She has fluffy feathers to keep her warm.

FUN FACTS ● FUN FACTS ● FUN FACTS ● FUN FACTS ● FUN FACTS

Penguins can jump out of the water, up into the air!

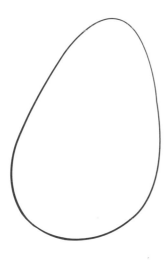

1. Draw this shape like a pointy egg.

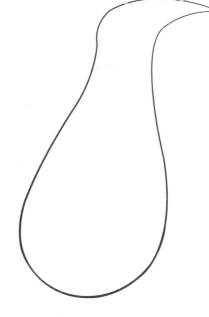

2. Put the head on with its long beak.

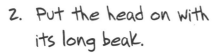

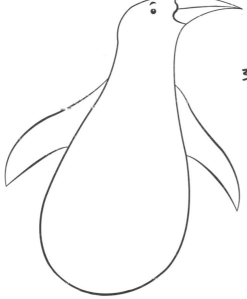

3. Her wings are like flippers.

4. She looks well dressed in black and white.

Scorpion

She curls her tail up over her back.

This scorpion's tail has a sting at the end.

She has big claws for grabbing hold of her food.

She has eight legs.

FUN FACTS ● FUN FACTS ● FUN FACTS ● FUN FACTS ● FUN FACTS

Mother scorpions look after their babies. They climb on her back and get a ride!

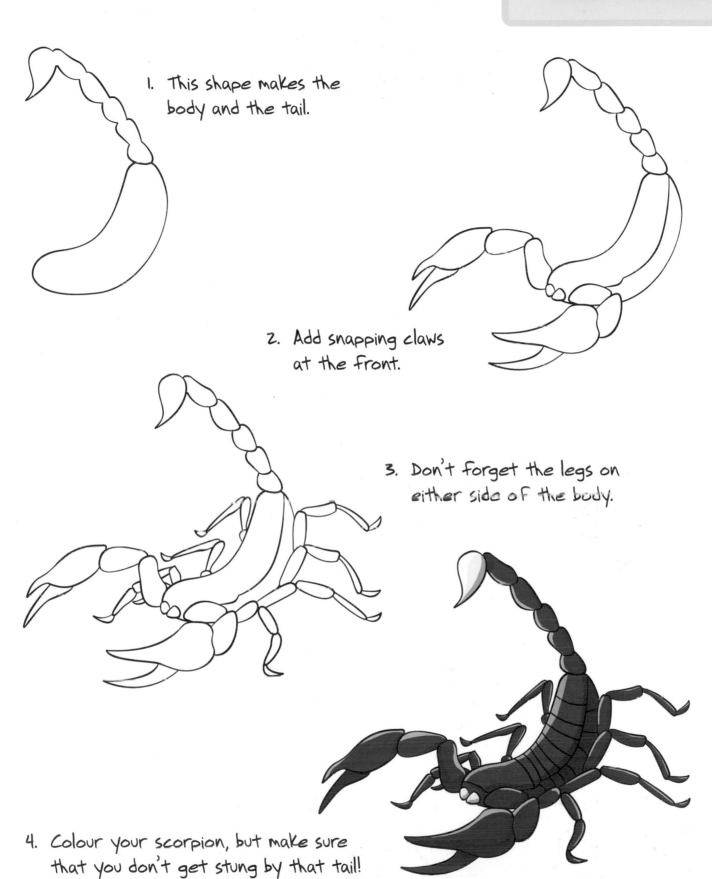

1. This shape makes the body and the tail.

2. Add snapping claws at the front.

3. Don't forget the legs on either side of the body.

4. Colour your scorpion, but make sure that you don't get stung by that tail!

Capture this hang glider soaring through the sky.

Draw this tennis player about to serve an ace.

Where do you think this roller skater is heading to?

Try to get the proportions of the horse and rider just right.

SPORTS PEOPLE

Get ready for the big match! People can be tricky to draw, especially when they're moving around! Improve your figure drawing skills by practising on these high-energy sports people in action poses.

Tennis player

A tennis player hits the ball with a bat called a racket.

He can hit the ball soft or hard.

He hits the ball over a net.

Tennis shoes help him turn and run fast.

FUN FACTS ● FUN FACTS ● FUN FACTS ● FUN FACTS ● FUN FACTS

Some players hit the ball very hard. It travels twice as fast as a car on a motorway!

1. Here's his body and head.

2. Now put in his arms and hands.

3. He's reaching up to serve the ball.

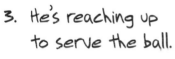

4. He dresses mostly in white.

Horse rider

The riding hat protects the rider if she falls.

She guides the horse using these reins.

The rider speaks to the horse.

She uses her feet to tell the horse to go fast or slow.

FUN FACTS ● FUN FACTS ● FUN FACTS ● FUN FACTS ● FUN FACTS

Horse riders sometimes play sports together. The winning horse and the rider may both get a medal!

1. Draw the horse's body and the rider's body.

2. Give the rider a hat. Start the horse's legs.

3. Now draw the other two legs.

4. Make the horse and the rider smile.

Hang glider

A hang glider is like a huge kite. It has one big wing.

The wind lifts it into the air.

The person flying the hang glider is called the pilot.

He makes the hang glider take off. He runs then jumps into the air.

FUN FACTS ● FUN FACTS ● FUN FACTS ● FUN FACTS ● FUN FACTS

Pilots can fly in their hang gliders for hours. They can travel hundreds of kilometres!

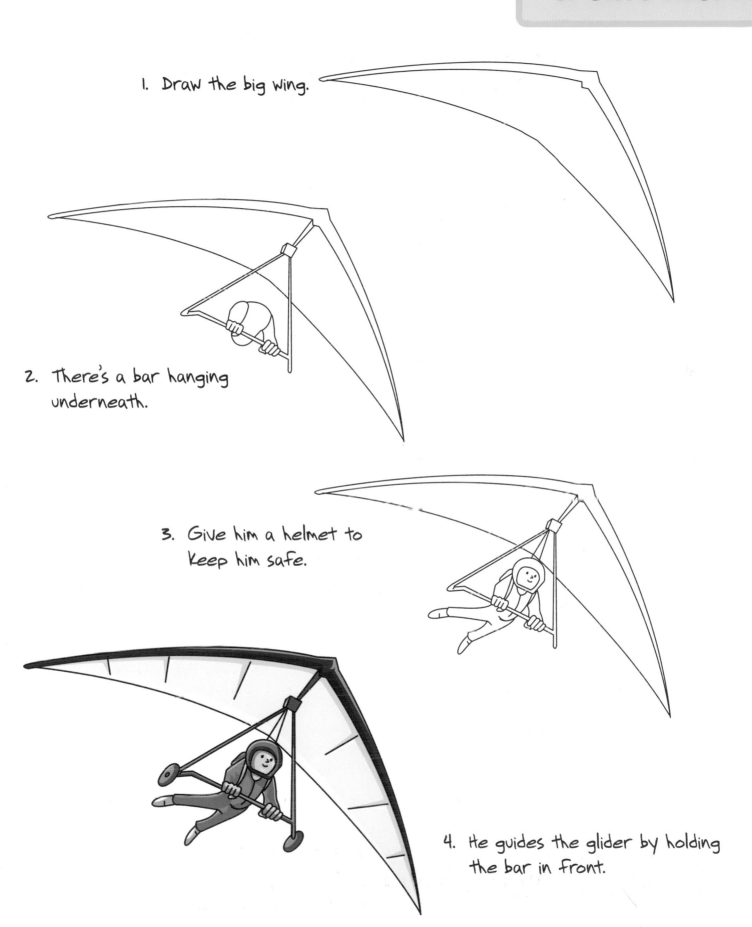

1. Draw the big wing.

2. There's a bar hanging underneath.

3. Give him a helmet to keep him safe.

4. He guides the glider by holding the bar in front.

Ice skater

An ice skater dances on ice.

The skater's arms and legs make pretty shapes.

She skates to music. She has to keep time.

Ice skates help the skater to spin and jump.

FUN FACTS ● FUN FACTS ● FUN FACTS ● FUN FACTS ● FUN FACTS

Some ice skaters dance on ice. Others have races or play a game called ice hockey!

1. Draw her two arms first.

2. Now add her head with her hair put up.

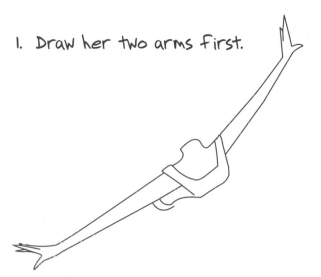

3. She's skating on one leg.

4. Give her a short skirt with lots of folds.

Roller skater

This skater wears a helmet on his head.

Some skates have two wheels at the front and two at the back.

These are called inline skates. The wheels are in a line.

He wears pads on his knees.

FUN FACTS ● FUN FACTS ● FUN FACTS ● FUN FACTS ● FUN FACTS

Roller skates were first used in a play. The play was in London, England, more than 250 years ago!

1. His body's quite thin.

2. He has long legs.

3. Draw his arms spread out for balance.

4. Give him elbow pads and a helmet in case he falls.

Deep-sea diver

The diver wears these flippers on his feet. They help him swim fast.

He carries a tank on his back. The tank is full of air.

He can stay under the water for around an hour.

He wears a diving suit. It stops him from getting cold.

FUN FACTS ● FUN FACTS ● FUN FACTS ● FUN FACTS ● FUN FACTS

Some divers don't wear air tanks. They are called free divers. Free divers can hold their breath for a long time.

1. Draw the body and helmet.

2. Next put on the arms.

3. He's got gloves and flippers.

4. He has his own air in a tank on his back.

Give this friendly cow some grass to chew on.

Changing the shape of the duck's bill will alter its expression.

Make this sheep's wool look nice and fluffy.

Can you get this happy pig's smile just right?

FARM ANIMALS

Now it's time to draw some more familiar animals - ones you might see on a trip to a farm. Try to give each animal its own personality. Perhaps you'll make your pig look happy or your donkey look proud.

Cow

FUN FACTS ● FUN FACTS ● FUN FACTS ● FUN FACTS ● FUN FACTS

Cows curl their tongues around grass to pull it up.

1. Her body is shaped like the Moon.

2. Now add on the legs and the head.

3. She has a big mouth for eating lots of grass.

4. Underneath are her udders.

sheep

This sheep has a woolly coat.

We use wool to make clothes.

Most sheep are white. They can also be black or brown.

She has short fur on her face and legs.

FUN FACTS ● FUN FACTS ● FUN FACTS ● FUN FACTS ● FUN FACTS

Sheep like to stay together. They always follow each other! A group of sheep is called a flock.

1. We start with a shape like a cloud.

2. Put the head at one end ...

3. ... and some legs underneath.

4. She has a woolly tail.

Chicken

She has a pointy yellow beak.

The red part on top of her head is called a comb.

She scrapes the ground with her feet. She looks for seeds and bugs to eat.

FUN FACTS ● FUN FACTS ● FUN FACTS ● FUN FACTS ● FUN FACTS

Chickens can fly. However they cannot fly very far.

1. Begin with this shape.

2. Her head goes at this end, her tail at the other.

3. Add a pair of strong, scratchy feet.

4. She has a red comb on her head.

Pig

This pig has big, pointy ears.

His skin is covered with short hairs.

He digs for food with his nose.

He likes to roll in the mud to keep cool.

FUN FACTS ● FUN FACTS ● FUN FACTS ● FUN FACTS ● FUN FACTS

Some people keep pigs as pets!

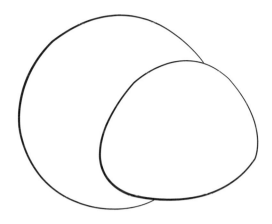

1. Draw two round shapes to start with.

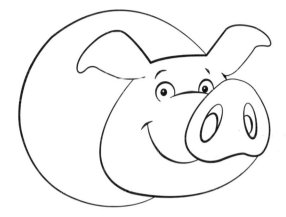

2. Add his ears, nose and eyes.

3. Now draw his legs.

4. Don't forget his curly tail!

Duck

This duck eats plants, fish and bugs.

She can use her wings to fly.

Ducks like to live near rivers and ponds.

She has webbed feet for swimming.

FUN FACTS ● FUN FACTS ● FUN FACTS ● FUN FACTS ● FUN FACTS

A duckling has a hard bump on its beak. This is called an egg tooth. It uses this to break out of its egg.

1. Draw this head, neck and body.

2. She has a big beak.

3. She's not swimming. She's standing on the ground.

4. Draw her big, orange webbed feet.

Donkey

This donkey has long pointy ears.

He has a thin, dark stripe along his back.

He is strong. He can carry heavy loads.

He can kick hard!

FUN FACTS ● FUN FACTS ● FUN FACTS ● FUN FACTS ● FUN FACTS

In some places, farmers keep donkeys with sheep.
The donkeys scare wolves away from the sheep!

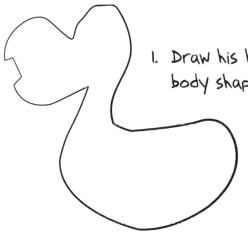

1. Draw his head and body shape.

2. He has very big ears.

3. Put three legs on the ground. The other leg is in the air.

4. He has a brown tail and shiny hooves.

Give this manga girl's dress a pretty pattern.

Use movement lines to show these hula hoops spinning around.

This manga boy is running very fast.

Manga characters often have brightly coloured hair.

MANGA CHARACTERS

This chapter is dedicated to the Japanese art form called manga. Manga artists draw distinctive looking characters. Follow the steps to learn how to draw them for yourself - but be sure to put your own spin on things!

Cute manga girl

Manga is the Japanese word for comic books. It is also a way of drawing.

Let's turn this girl into a manga drawing!

She stands in a cute way. She has her hand on her hip. Her eyes are wide open.

She is wearing a pretty dress and matching shoes.

FUN FACTS ● FUN FACTS ● FUN FACTS ● FUN FACTS ● FUN FACTS

Manga began in Japan more than 50 years ago. Now it is popular all over the world!

1. Start with her head and body.

2. Put in some long hair ...

3. ... and some more long hair.

4. She's wearing a pretty yellow dress.

Skateboarder

Manga stories are full of action. This skateboarder would make a great manga figure.

He has messy hair.

His skateboard has four wheels.

He wears baggy clothes. They let him move easily.

FUN FACTS ● FUN FACTS ● FUN FACTS ● FUN FACTS ● FUN FACTS

A skater can make the board jump into the air using only his feet. This famous trick is called an 'ollie'.

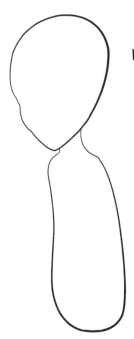

1. Begin with his head and body.

2. Make his hair a bit messy.

3. He's carrying a skateboard.

4. Finish off with his legs.

Girl and cat

Here is another cute picture. Manga figures are often cute.

This girl loves her cat. It's friendly and fun to play with.

She picks it up and strokes it.

It likes being stroked. It purrs when it's happy.

FUN FACTS ● FUN FACTS ● FUN FACTS ● FUN FACTS ● FUN FACTS

Some manga stories are about animals that act like people. A famous manga movie is called 'The Cat Returns'.

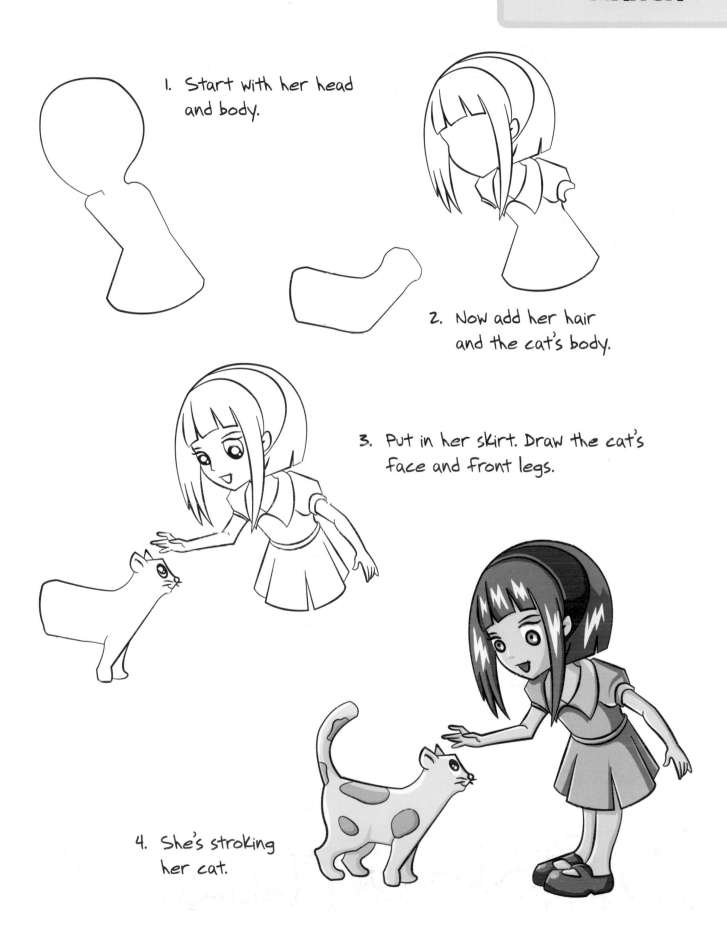

1. Start with her head and body.

2. Now add her hair and the cat's body.

3. Put in her skirt. Draw the cat's face and front legs.

4. She's stroking her cat.

Runner

This boy is running fast.

He wears shorts and a T-shirt. These let his arms and legs move easily.

He uses his arms to help him run.

He runs in bare feet. However top runners wear running shoes.

FUN FACTS ● FUN FACTS ● FUN FACTS ● FUN FACTS ● FUN FACTS

The fastest men on Earth run 100 metres (109 yards) in less than ten seconds. That's fast!

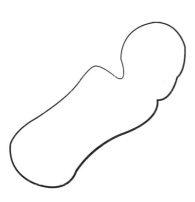

1. Draw the head and body.

2. Put in his hair and his shirt.

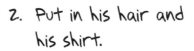

3. Now add his face and his running legs.

4. Finish off with his arms and feet.

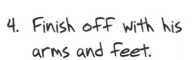

Hula hoop girl

A hula hoop is fun to play with.

This girl makes her body go round in circles. This makes the hula hoop spin.

To keep it spinning, she has to move really fast.

Sometimes, people spin several hula hoops at the same time.

FUN FACTS ● FUN FACTS ● FUN FACTS ● FUN FACTS ● FUN FACTS

People try to spin the hula hoop for as long as they can. The longest spin ever lasted over three and a half days!

1. Here's her head and body.

2. Put in her hair and arms.

3. Add her face.

4. She's playing with hoops.

Skipping rope

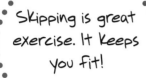

Skipping is great exercise. It keeps you fit!

The boy skips forwards. He brings the rope over his head from the back.

He can skip on the spot. Or he can run and skip at the same time.

He can also skip backwards. He brings the rope over from the front.

FUN FACTS ● FUN FACTS ● FUN FACTS ● FUN FACTS ● FUN FACTS

In 1995, a man ran a marathon race while skipping all the way!

1. Draw the head and body.

2. In manga drawings, people often have spiky hair.

3. Put in the arms and legs.

4. Finish off with the skipping rope.

Girl in the rain

She has an umbrella. It keeps the rain off her.

This girl wears a raincoat to keep her dry.

She wears boots for splashing in the puddles.

Walking in the rain is fun if you wear the right clothes!

FUN FACTS ● FUN FACTS ● FUN FACTS ● FUN FACTS ● FUN FACTS

The first umbrellas were used to protect people from the sun, not the rain.

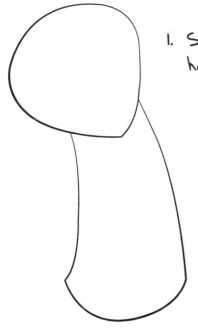

1. Start with her head and body.

2. Now put on her hair and a coat.

3. She has a hat ...

4. ... and a colourful umbrella.

Archer

This archer shoots with a bow and arrow.

She aims carefully.

She pulls back the string to shoot the arrow.

The arrow flies fast through the air.

FUN FACTS ● FUN FACTS ● FUN FACTS ● FUN FACTS ● FUN FACTS

An arrow flies through the air very fast. It travels about twice as fast as a car on a motorway!

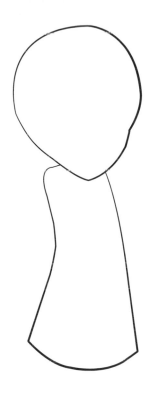

1. Start with her head and body.

2. Put in her face and hair.

3. Add her clothes and arms.

4. She has a bow and arrows.

FANTASY CHARACTERS

You'll meet some really crazy characters in this fantastic chapter. Whether it's fire-breathing dragons, brave superheroes or terrifying giants, there are lots of cool things to draw in here!

Superhero

Superheroes help people who are in danger.

Superheroes have amazing powers. Some can fly.

Many superheroes wear capes.

Superheroes are very strong. Some are so strong they can lift a car!

FUN FACTS ● FUN FACTS ● FUN FACTS ● FUN FACTS ● FUN FACTS

The most famous superhero of all is called Superman. The first Superman comic book appeared in 1938.

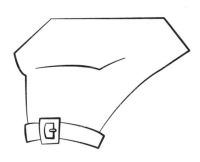

1. Draw his body.

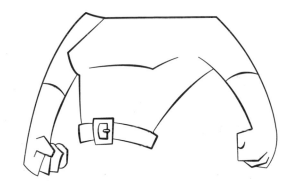

2. Add his strong arms.

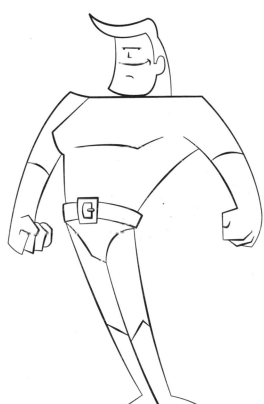

3. Now put in his head and legs.

4. This superhero has a big cape!

Dragon

A dragon is a huge monster that can fly.

It has a neck like a snake.

It can breathe fire! It uses the fire to scare people away.

It has a body like a huge lizard. It also has big wings.

FUN FACTS ● FUN FACTS ● FUN FACTS ● FUN FACTS ● FUN FACTS

In many stories, dragons are bad. However in China, dragons are meant to bring happiness and good luck!

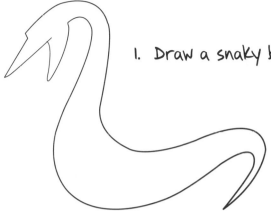

1. Draw a snaky body shape.

2. Put in the spiky head.

3. He has four legs.

4. His wings are out. He's breathing fire!

Queen

A queen is a woman who rules a country.

The queen is rich. She wears lots of jewels.

She looks very important. She tells people what to do!

She wears a dress that costs a lot of money.

FUN FACTS ● FUN FACTS ● FUN FACTS ● FUN FACTS ● FUN FACTS

One famous queen from history was Elizabeth I of England. She was very powerful and never got married.

1. She has a very curvy body.

2. Draw her puff sleeves and big skirt.

3. Give her a little crown, but a huge collar.

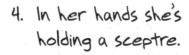

4. In her hands she's holding a sceptre.

Giant

Giants are big but they are not very smart.

They sometimes try to eat people.

Giants like fighting. This one is carrying a huge club.

He has a necklace made of bones.

FUN FACTS ● FUN FACTS ● FUN FACTS ● FUN FACTS ● FUN FACTS

There is a giant in the story of Jack and the Beanstalk. The giant lives in a castle on a cloud.

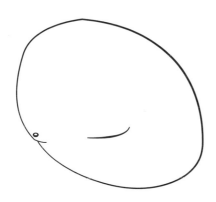

1. Draw a big, round body.

2. Add the head and legs.

3. Put in the arms and the big club.

4. Colour the club like a piece of wood.

Troll

A troll is a horrible, ugly monster.

This troll has a big club.

Trolls never wash. They smell really bad.

Trolls sometimes live under bridges.

FUN FACTS ● FUN FACTS ● FUN FACTS ● FUN FACTS ● FUN FACTS

In some stories, trolls are scared of sunlight. If they go out in sunlight, they turn to stone!

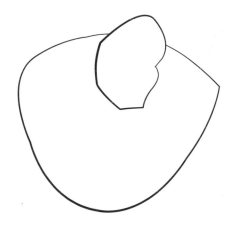

1. Draw a big, wide body.

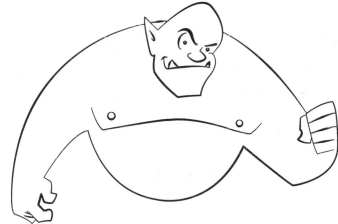

2. Give him sharp teeth and ears.

3. He has two small legs.

4. In his hand he carries a club with nails in it.

DINOSAURS

Nobody knows exactly what dinosaurs looked like, so you can let your imagination run wild! Were they dull and drab or bright and colourful? You decide!

Allosaurus

aa-luh-SOHR-uhs

Allosaurus was a meat-eating dinosaur.

Allosaurus was a big dinosaur, almost 12 metres (about 38 feet) long.

It had about 60 very sharp teeth.

It used its front claws to hold on to prey.

FUN FACTS ● FUN FACTS ● FUN FACTS ● FUN FACTS ● FUN FACTS

Allosaurus ate other dinosaurs. It tried to creep close to them. Then it suddenly attacked.

1. This shape makes the body and the tail.

2. Add the neck and head.

3. Short front arms and eyebrows are next.

4. Powerful back legs finish off this frightening animal.

Apatosaurus

ah-pah-tuh-SOHR-uhs

This huge dinosaur was about 21 metres (70 feet) long.

Its neck was very long to reach its food.

It ate leaves and bushes growing near the ground.

It used its tail like a whip if a meat-eating dinosaur attacked it.

FUN FACTS ● FUN FACTS ● FUN FACTS ● FUN FACTS ● FUN FACTS

Apatosaurus lived in groups so the adults could keep the babies safe.

1. This shape is the body.

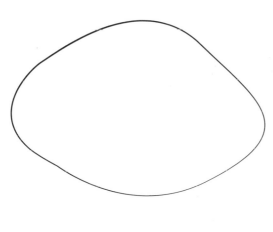

2. Make the neck long and smooth.

3. Put on the head and a long, strong tail.

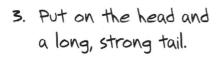

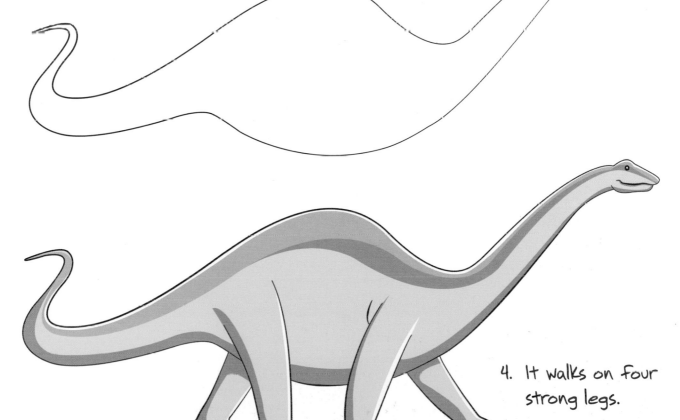

4. It walks on four strong legs.

Deinonychus

dy-NAH-nih-kuhs

This dinosaur had sharp eyes for spotting prey.

Its tail was used for balance as it ran.

It had large claws on its back feet.

Deinonychus was about 3 metres (10 feet) long.

FUN FACTS ● FUN FACTS ● FUN FACTS ● FUN FACTS ● FUN FACTS

Deinonychus hunted in groups. Together they could kill animals much bigger than themselves.

1. Draw a long body to start.

2. Add in the head.

3. Give it two small front legs.

4. Add the back legs, then draw its teeth and claws.

Parasaurolophus

pa-ruh-sohr-uh-LOH-fus

This dinosaur had a huge crest on its head.

Parasaurolophus probably lived in groups.

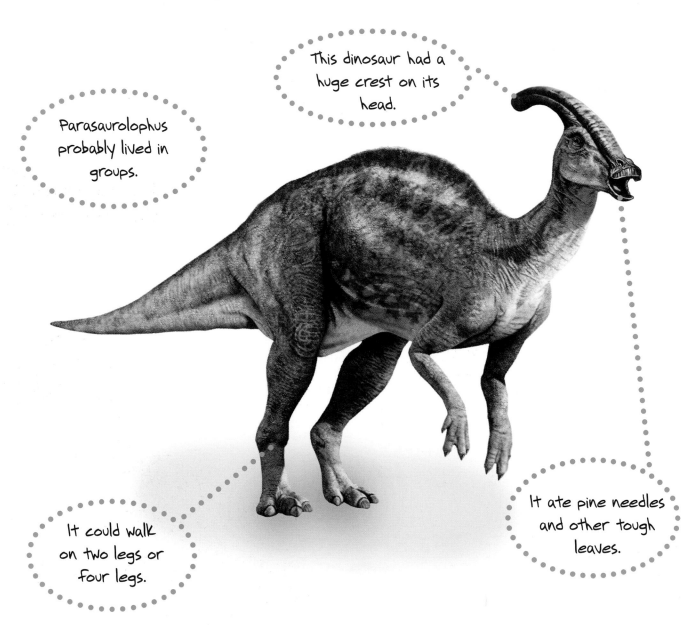

It ate pine needles and other tough leaves.

It could walk on two legs or four legs.

FUN FACTS ● FUN FACTS ● FUN FACTS ● FUN FACTS ● FUN FACTS

Parasaurolophus could blow through its crest. This made a loud, low noise.

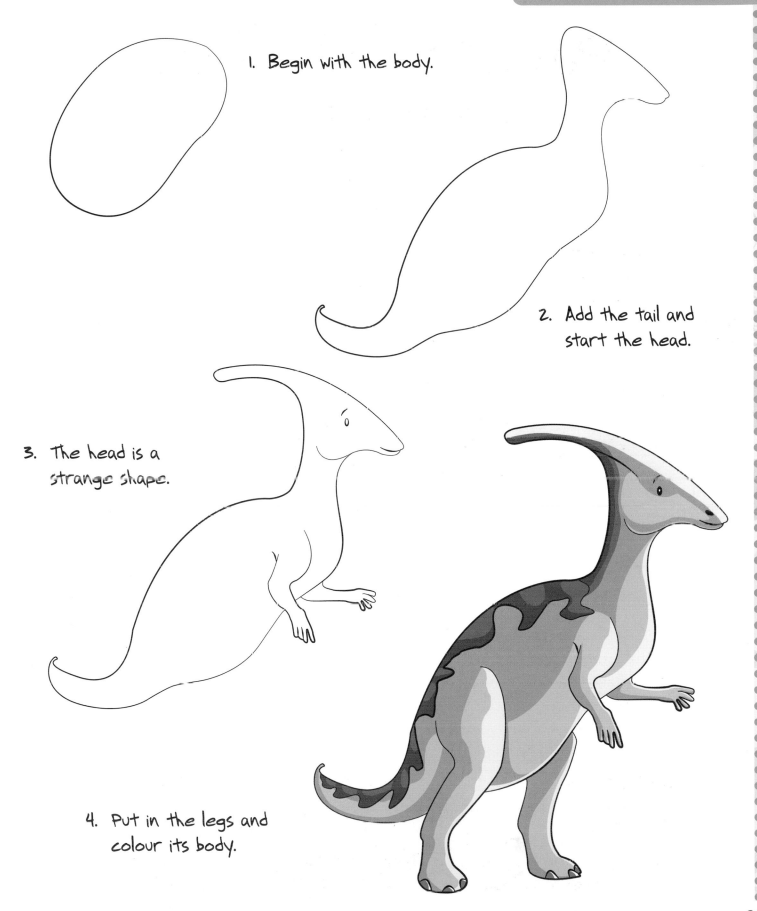

1. Begin with the body.

2. Add the tail and start the head.

3. The head is a strange shape.

4. Put in the legs and colour its body.

Spinosaurus

spy-nuh-SOHR-uhs

Spinosaurus was a meat-eating dinosaur.

The 'sail' on its back was taller than a person.

It was more than 11 metres (35 feet) long.

It snapped up fish with its sharp teeth.

FUN FACTS ● FUN FACTS ● FUN FACTS ● FUN FACTS ● FUN FACTS

Spinosaurus used its sail to keep warm. It stood so the sun shone on its sail. This warmed it up very quickly.

1. Begin with this shape for the body.

2. Add a head with a long mouth, and a powerful tail at the other end.

3. A spiny sail on its back and sharp teeth and claws are next.

4. Now add in the legs. It looks like you may be next for lunch!

Archaeopteryx

ahr-kee-AHP-tuh-rihks

This was one of the first birds. It lived at the time of the dinosaurs.

It had feathers like a modern bird.

It could not fly well, but used its wings to glide.

These claws helped it climb around in trees.

FUN FACTS ● FUN FACTS ● FUN FACTS ● FUN FACTS ● FUN FACTS

Archaeopteryx was about the size of a pigeon.

1. Draw the body with a feathery tail.

2. Add the head and one large wing.

3. Now add the other wing.

4. Finish it off with legs and clawed feet.

VEHICLES

Whether it travels by road,
rail or flies through the sky, you'll find the
vehicle for you in this chapter. Try to get
your drawings as accurate as possible - down to
the final nut and bolt!

Car

The engine is at the front. It is under a lid called the bonnet.

This car is very comfortable to sit inside.

At night, lights show the driver where he is going.

The tyres are filled with air.

FUN FACTS ● FUN FACTS ● FUN FACTS ● FUN FACTS ● FUN FACTS

The fastest car in the world is called Thrust SSC. This car looks like a rocket but it has wheels.

1. This will be a smooth, streamlined shape.

2. Draw the windows and spaces for the wheels.

3. More lines show the shape.

4. Colour the edges lighter to make it look shiny.

Bicycle

A rider makes the bicycle move by turning the pedals.

She pulls the brakes to stop. They make the wheels stop turning.

The pedals turn a chain. The chain then turns the back wheel.

The front wheel is pushed along by the back wheel.

FUN FACTS ● FUN FACTS ● FUN FACTS ● FUN FACTS ● FUN FACTS

The most famous bicycle race is called the Tour de France. The riders in this race travel around France.

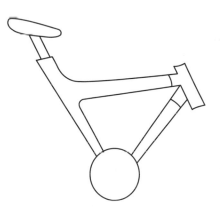

1. The first part is like a triangle.

2. Put in the handlebar and pedals.

3. You could trace around something to do the wheels.

4. Now add some colour to finish it off.

Sports Car

The engine is in the middle of the car, behind the seats.

This sports car has tinted windows, to keep it cool inside.

The tyres have excellent grip.

The front bumper protects the car.

FUN FACTS ● FUN FACTS ● FUN FACTS ● FUN FACTS ● FUN FACTS

The fastest car in the world is the Hennessy Venom GT. It can reach speeds of over 430 kph (270 mph)!

1. Draw this shape with smooth lines.

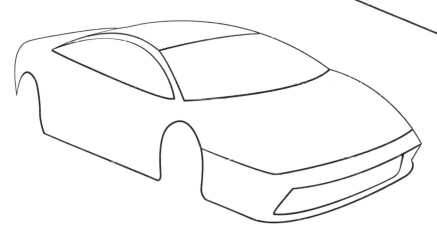

2. Add the windows and spaces where the wheels will go.

3. Draw in some more details, like the wheels and doors.

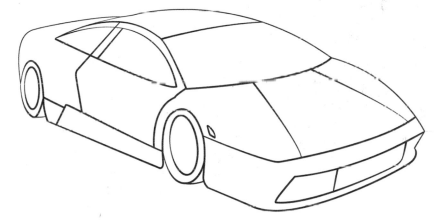

4. Paint it a bright colour so it'll really stand out on the road!

Bus

This bus is long and narrow.

The bus has big mirrors. They help the driver see around the bus.

Everyone's bags go in here.

On some buses, you can watch TV as you travel!

FUN FACTS ● FUN FACTS ● FUN FACTS ● FUN FACTS ● FUN FACTS

Some buses have two decks. Sometimes the top deck has no roof. The people sit in the open air!

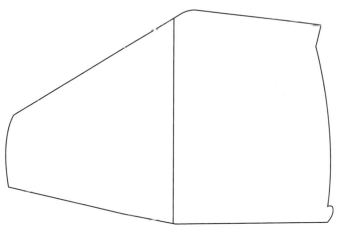

1. We'll start with a large box shape.

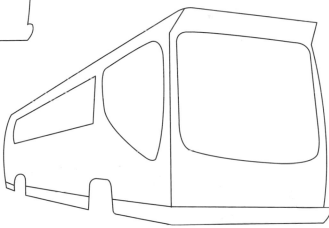

2. Now put in the big windows.

3. Lines show where the doors are.

4. Give it blue windows.

Train

A train carries lots of people. The people get on and off at stations.

The driver looks through this window.

Trains cannot travel up or down steep hills.

It has wheels that travel on rails.

FUN FACTS ● FUN FACTS ● FUN FACTS ● FUN FACTS ● FUN FACTS

The train was invented in England around 200 years ago!

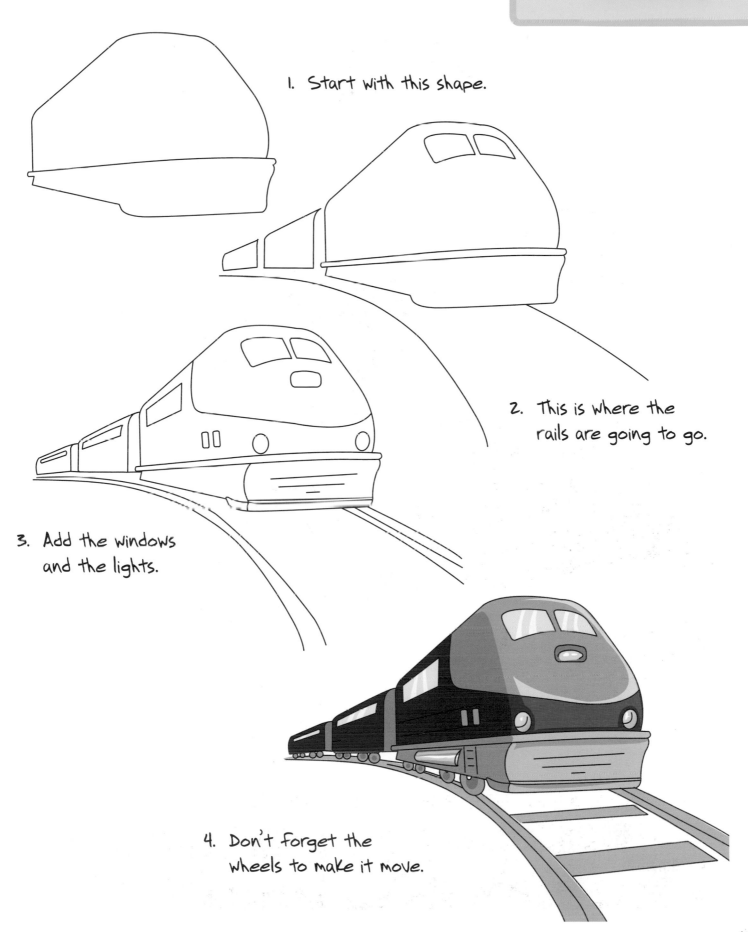

1. Start with this shape.

2. This is where the rails are going to go.

3. Add the windows and the lights.

4. Don't forget the wheels to make it move.

Motorbike

This motorbike is small and light. However it has a powerful engine.

People use motorbikes for getting around quickly.

Some motorbikes are used for racing.

You can see the engine.

FUN FACTS ● FUN FACTS ● FUN FACTS ● FUN FACTS ● FUN FACTS

The motorbike is one of the world's most common vehicles.
There are over 200 million of them!

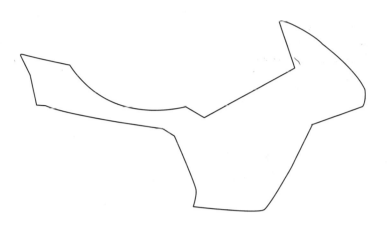

1. First, draw the body of the motorbike.

2. It has three parts.

3. Add the seat, the front fork and the pipe at the back.

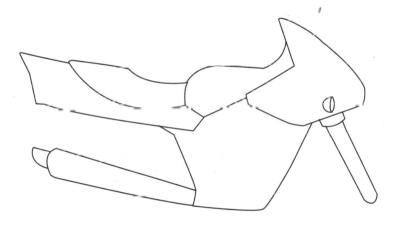

4. Now add the wheels. You can also show the end of the handlebar.

Kart

The engine is at the back of the kart.

These pedals make the kart go faster or stop.

Bumpers keep the driver from being hurt if a kart crashes.

Karts have small, thick wheels.

FUN FACTS • FUN FACTS • FUN FACTS • FUN FACTS • FUN FACTS

Many top racing drivers began by racing karts. There are races for kart drivers as young as eight.

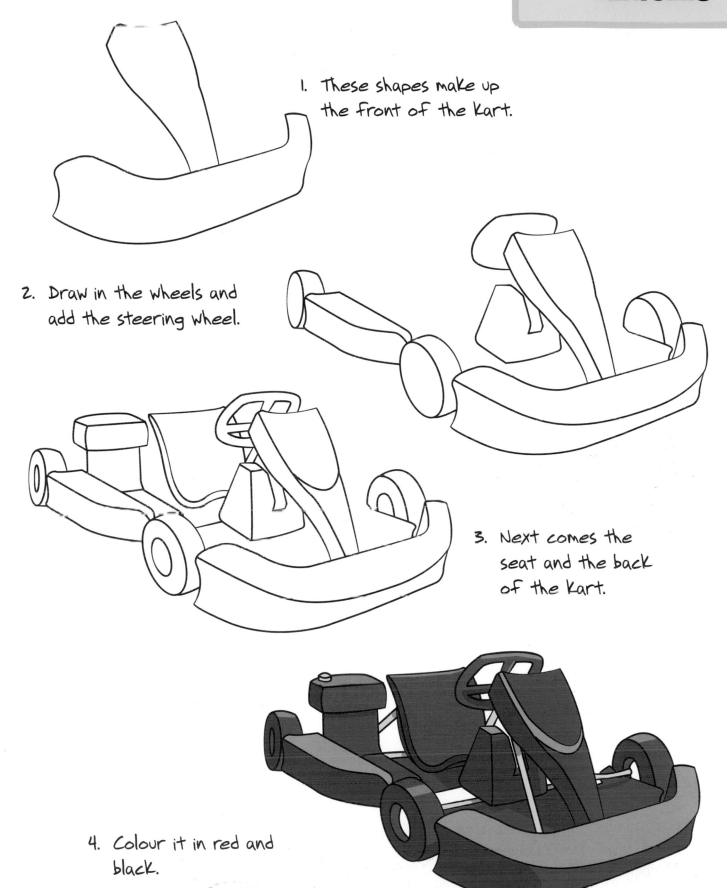

1. These shapes make up the front of the kart.

2. Draw in the wheels and add the steering wheel.

3. Next comes the seat and the back of the kart.

4. Colour it in red and black.

Jet plane

This plane has two engines. An engine is a machine that makes something move.

Big planes carry hundreds of people.

It has long wings. The wings help it lift into the air.

It has wheels underneath for taking off and landing.

FUN FACTS ● FUN FACTS ● FUN FACTS ● FUN FACTS ● FUN FACTS

A jet plane must move forwards to stay in the air. It cannot stop or fly backwards.

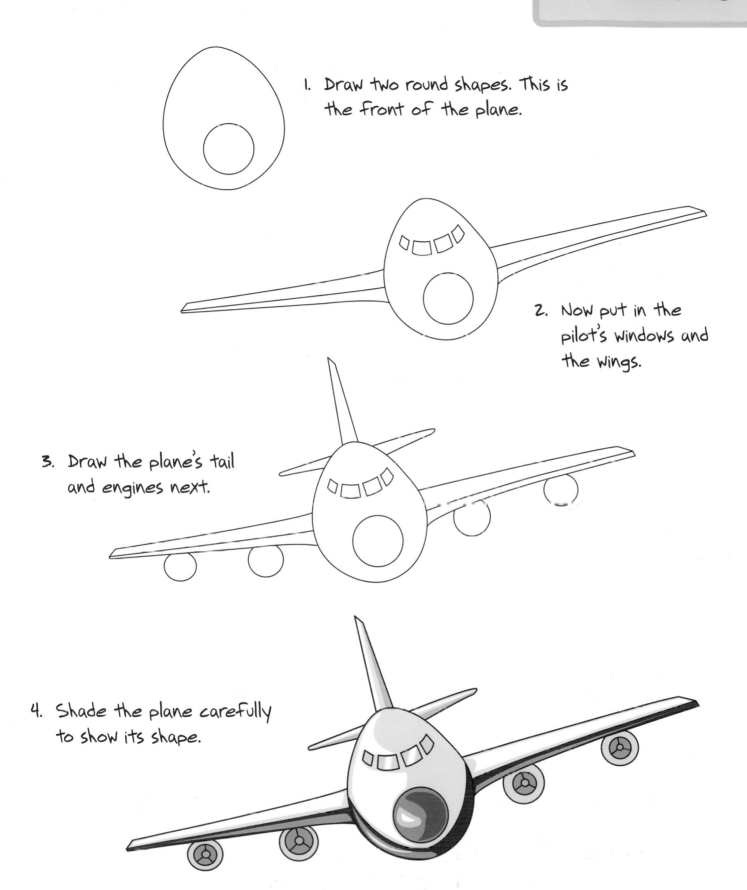

1. Draw two round shapes. This is the front of the plane.

2. Now put in the pilot's windows and the wings.

3. Draw the plane's tail and engines next.

4. Shade the plane carefully to show its shape.

Helicopter

Most helicopters carry only a few people at a time.

These long blades spin round. They lift the helicopter into the air.

The tail helps it to fly in the right direction.

When it takes off it rises straight up. When it lands, it goes straight down.

FUN FACTS ● FUN FACTS ● FUN FACTS ● FUN FACTS ● FUN FACTS

A helicopter can fly forwards and backwards. It can also fly in one spot!

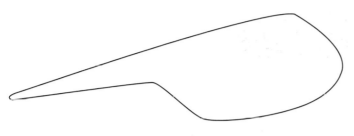

1. This is the body and tail.

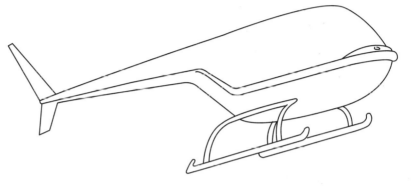

2. Finish the tail and add some runners.

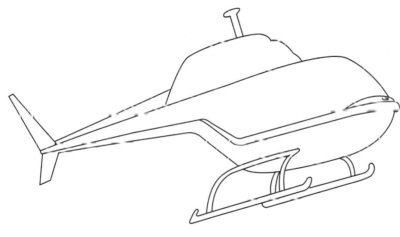

3. The bit on the top has the engine inside.

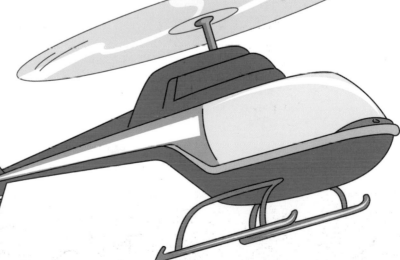

4. The blades go so fast, they look like a circle.

Stunt Plane

A biplane has one wing on top and one wing below.

It has space for two people.

Biplanes have shorter wings than ordinary planes.

The propeller moves the plane forwards through the air.

FUN FACTS ● FUN FACTS ● FUN FACTS ● FUN FACTS ● FUN FACTS

Planes with propellers are good at flying at slow speeds. People can easily see as the plane twists and turns in the air.

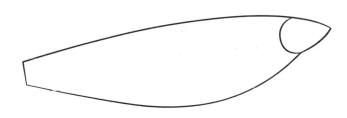

1. Start with a curved shape for the body.

2. Add in the two wings.

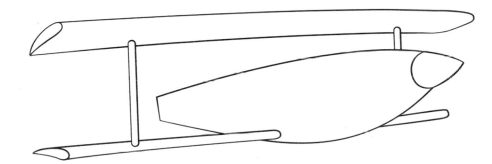

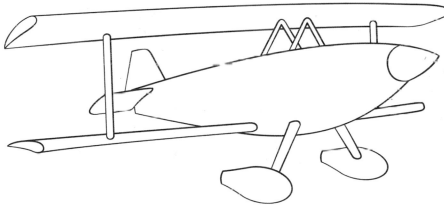

3. Now it's starting to look more like a plane.

4. Add a propeller and choose bright colours to make the plane fly off the page.

Draw this hammerhead shark diving down into the sea.

This chunky walrus looks very pleased with itself.

Capture this jellyfish gently drifting with the current.

Try to make the sailfish's nose as sharp as possible.

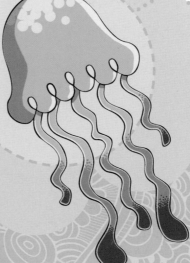

SEA CREATURES

Let's head below the waves to draw these super sea creatures. From the giant walrus and spiky sailfish to the long-legged octopus, there are lots of cool critters down here for you to recreate!

Walrus

This walrus is very fat. This keeps him warm in the cold sea.

He has long tusks.

His back flippers are strong to push him through the water. He steers with his front flippers.

He is big, about 4.3 metres (14 feet) long.

FUN FACTS ● FUN FACTS ● FUN FACTS ● FUN FACTS ● FUN FACTS

Walruses are good swimmers. They dive down to the ocean floor and eat the small animals they find there.

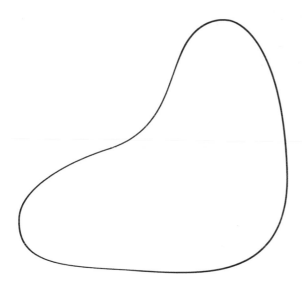

1. Draw a large blob for the body.

2. Add a round, smiling face.

3. Draw long tusks, then begin his flippers.

4. Finish off the flippers, then colour your walrus.

Jellyfish

This jellyfish has a soft, wobbly body.

The top of the jellyfish is called the bell.

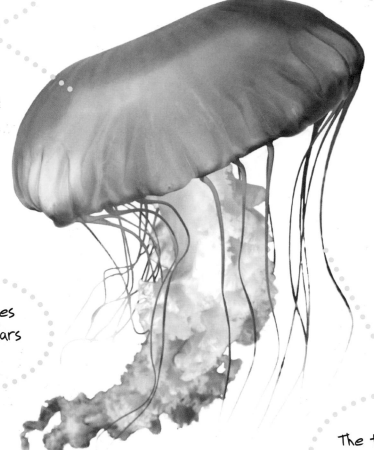

The jellyfish does not have eyes, ears or a brain.

The tentacles look like hair – but they can sting!

FUN FACTS ● FUN FACTS ● FUN FACTS ● FUN FACTS ● FUN FACTS

Some jellyfish can sting even after they have died.

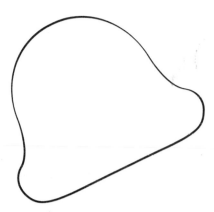

1. A basic bell shape begins the body.

2. Draw some curves along the bottom.

3. Add lots of wavy tentacles for catching prey.

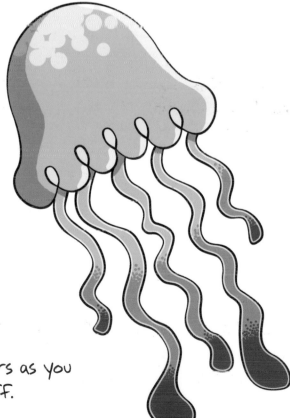

4. Use as many colours as you like to finish it off.

Sailfish

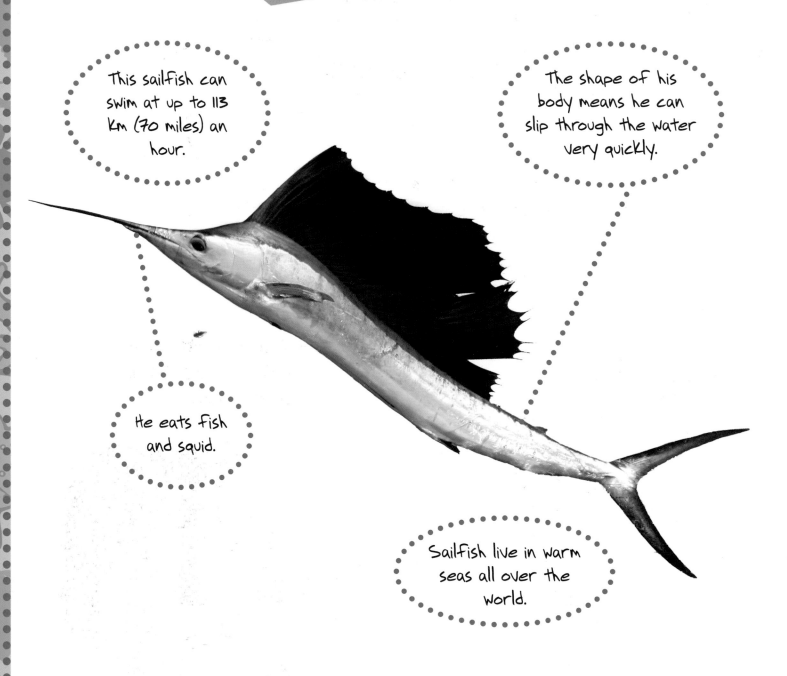

This sailfish can swim at up to 113 km (70 miles) an hour.

The shape of his body means he can slip through the water very quickly.

He eats fish and squid.

Sailfish live in warm seas all over the world.

FUN FACTS ● FUN FACTS ● FUN FACTS ● FUN FACTS ● FUN FACTS

Female sailfish lay millions of eggs, but many animals eat them. Only a few will grow into adult sailfish.

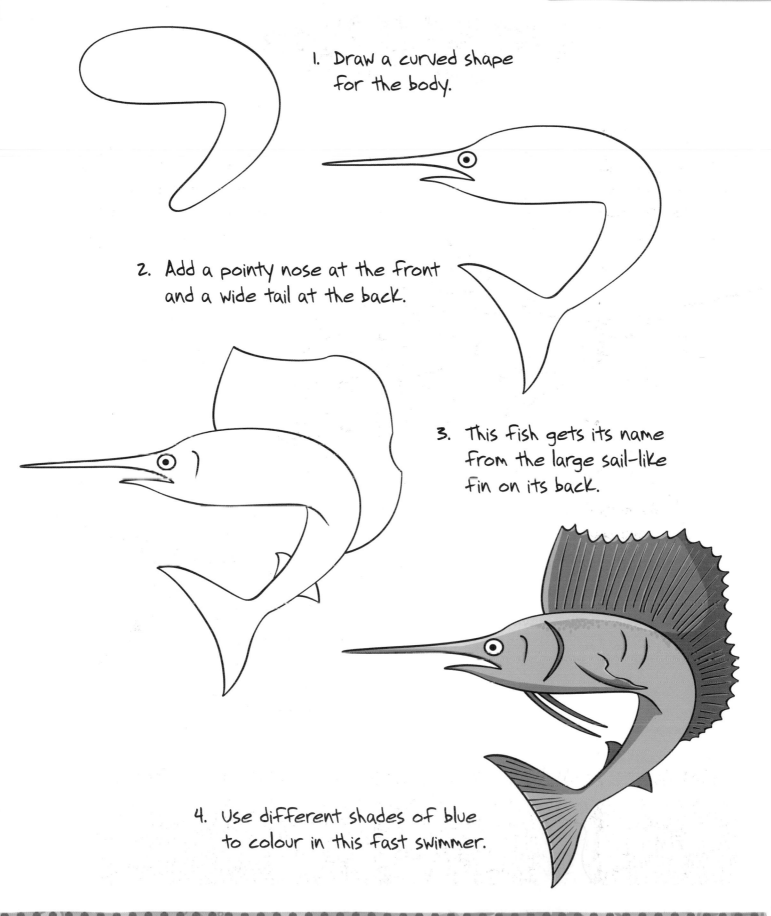

1. Draw a curved shape for the body.

2. Add a pointy nose at the front and a wide tail at the back.

3. This fish gets its name from the large sail-like fin on its back.

4. Use different shades of blue to colour in this fast swimmer.

Hammerhead shark

This hammerhead shark has an eye on either side of his 'hammer'.

He sometimes swims in a group with other hammerheads.

He eats fish, small sharks and stingrays.

He is 6 metres (20 feet) long.

FUN FACTS ● FUN FACTS ● FUN FACTS ● FUN FACTS ● FUN FACTS

Why do these sharks have weird-shaped heads? The hammer helps them to see in all directions.

1. Draw a simple curved shape for the body.

2. Add a tail and a hammer-shaped head.

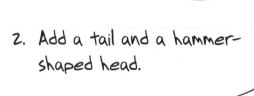

3. Wide, flat fins make him look more like a shark.

4. Colour him in dark blue or grey.

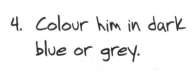

Octopus

This octopus has a soft body and eight arms.

She swims by squirting water out of her body.

Her bite is poisonous. She eats fish, snails and turtles.

If she is in danger, she can squirt ink into the water and escape.

FUN FACTS ● FUN FACTS ● FUN FACTS ● FUN FACTS ● FUN FACTS

The blue-ringed octopus lives in Australia. Its bite can kill a person in just a few minutes.

1. This shape gives you the body and two arms.

2. Add two eyes and more arms.

3. Draw still more arms – you need eight in total.

4. Add suckers on the arms. Then colour her in any way you want.